# A Little Bit of Help

## Megan and Simon

# A LITTLE BIT OF HELP — REVISED EDITION
## © 2025 Simon Robinson

All text, educational design, and page layouts are the intellectual property of the authors. Illustrations and supporting images were created or directed by the authors using licensed AI tools and original educational artwork.

All rights reserved. No part of this publication may be reproduced, stored, or transmitted in any form or by any means—electronic, mechanical, photocopying, recording, or otherwise—without prior written permission from the publisher, except for brief quotations in critical articles or reviews, or for classroom use within educational fair-use guidelines.

This revised edition supersedes earlier versions previously distributed through Amazon Kindle Direct Publishing.

Published by Dr Simon Robinson, Scarborough, North Yorkshire UK.
Printed and distributed by IngramSpark in the United Kingdom, United States, and Australia.

ISBN 978-1-0684310-5-0

Revised Edition 2025

## Educational Acknowledgement
This book was created as part of the Megan Learning Series, integrating literacy, numeracy, and social understanding for young adult learners.
Vocabulary lists, learning cards, and companion resources are available at drsimonrobinson.com/learning-cards.

## Image & Design Credits
All illustrations generated or adapted via AI under the direction of the authors. No corporate trademarks are reproduced; all brand likenesses are educational or generic renderings.

Cover and interior design by Dr Simon Robinson.
Educational annotations © Simon Robinson 2025.

**Typography & Production**
Set in *Spectral, Georgia, Crimson Text,* and *Patrick Hand,*
licensed under the SIL Open Font License v1.1.
Typeset and designed in Affinity Publisher and Affinity Designer.
Printed in the United Kingdom by IngramSpark.

**Library & Legal Information**
A CIP record for this title is available from the British Library.
Legal deposit copies will be lodged with the British Library and relevant UK Libraries Act partners.

**Publisher**
Dr Simon Robinson
Scarborough, North Yorkshire, UK
drsimonrobinson.com | wordbotherers.com
contact@drsimonrobinson.com

**Colophon**
The first edition of *A Little Bit of Help* was completed in Scarborough, North Yorkshire, and printed through IngramSpark in the United Kingdom, the United States, and Australia. Earlier draft versions were circulated privately for educational testing. This revised edition represents the definitive text and design of the *Megan Learning Series* Vol. 1.

Continue Megan's journey in *All By Myself.*

# Contents

| | |
|---|---|
| Hello | 9 |
| A little bit of help | 11 |
| Words | 13 |
| The Calendar | 15 |
| My Show | 17 |
| Going to the Tip | 19 |
| My Watch | 21 |
| Youtube | 23 |
| Tidying my bedroom | 25 |
| Looking down | 27 |
| Opposites | 29 |
| Flowers | 31 |
| Emotions | 33 |
| Colours | 35 |
| Shapes | 37 |

| | |
|---|---|
| MAPS | 39 |
| THE FIVE SENSES | 41 |
| FRACTIONS | 43 |
| DIFFERENT TYPES OF CARS | 45 |
| A STORY ABOUT BEER | 47 |
| SHOPPING | 49 |
| "NO, IT'S WRONG!" | 51 |
| NEW SANDALS | 53 |
| TAKE AWAY | 55 |
| BEING TIRED | 57 |
| LAUNDRY | 59 |
| THE THIRD DIGIT | 61 |
| SIXTY | 63 |
| TOO HOT | 65 |
| THE WEATHER | 67 |
| MY NEW TELEVISION | 69 |
| TAKING A LOOK AT THE CAR | 71 |
| MY NEW WARDROBE | 73 |

# INTRODUCTION

Megan has learning disabilities — we have been helping her with her language skills. Once she learns something new, she can remember it, but this takes time. During the Covid lockdowns, we had plenty of time and started by teaching her some basic concepts.

The main purpose of this book is to help Megan improve her reading. Many of the books suitable for her reading level are primarily designed for children. To help with her engagement, we decided to write the book together and create stories that are relevant to her daily life.

Megan has contributed where she can. She has only recently started using complete sentences and is beginning to learn about grammar and tense.

Despite relatively slow progress, Megan is making progress, and her comprehension is improving daily. This is inspiration enough!

# HELLO

My name is Megan.

Also, Simon is helping me write this book.

I am from Yorkshire.

My favourite meal is fish, chips, and mushy peas.

I like to watch the news.

I hope you like my book.

We are writing this to help me learn to read.

# A LITTLE BIT OF HELP

When I help Mum cook, I can only help a little bit.

Some of the jobs I help Mum with are :
1. helping Mum carry the shopping from the car and then putting it away;
2. sometimes I get our dog some chicken;
3. I help Mum load and empty the dishwasher;
4. and sometimes I clean the kitchen.

Now I am helping Mum with the laundry.

I hope I can learn to be even more helpful.

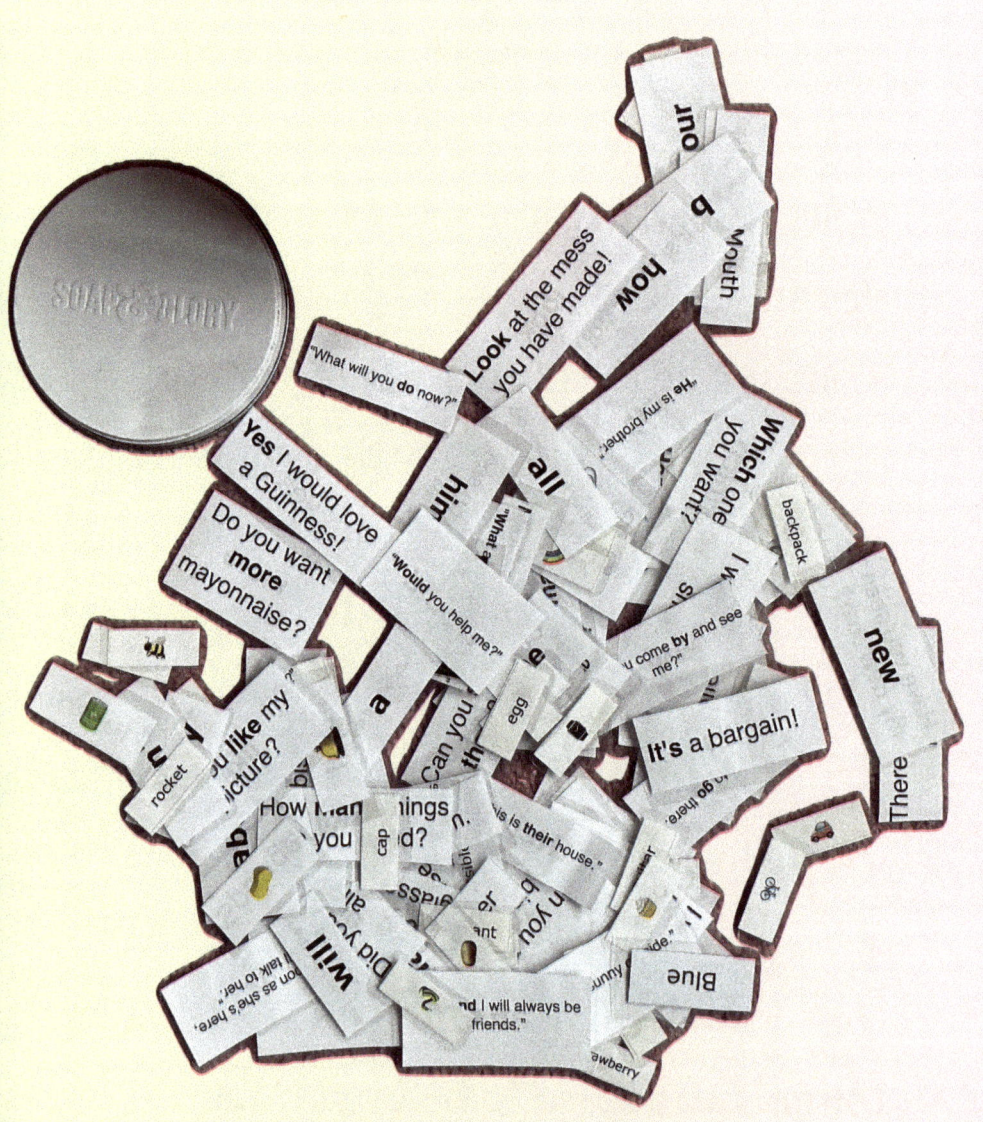

MY WORD CARDS AND TIN

# WORDS

"*I can do it!*", Megan says when she reads a whole sentence by herself.

Every day we try to sit down and learn words. We have a metal tin which is half-full of cards with words and sentences printed on them.

We also have some cards with pictures on them and the word on the back.

Sometimes Megan is too tired to learn words.

We have been learning to read words for almost two years.

Do you enjoy learning words Megan?

"*Yes I do*" she replies.

**30** days has
September, April, June,
and November.
All the rest have 31.
But February's 28.
The leap year,
which comes once in
four.
Gives February one
day more.

A POEM TO HELP REMEMBER THE
DAYS IN EACH MONTH

# THE CALENDAR

First, I learned about the days.

Then, the months.

After I remembered the names of the months , I learned their order.

Now we are learning how many days each month has.

I am very good at remembering birthdays and use my phone's calendar app to help me.

"Yes I do," says Megan.

WAITING FOR THE SHOW TO START

# My Show

Next week, on the twenty-eighth, I am in a show.

My show is about different places and people. There will be singing and dancing.

This is not my first show.

We do a new show every year at my college. I have friends and family coming to watch me dance.

They have bought seats for the front row.

Our dog isn't coming.

"He has to stay all alone by himself," says Megan.

SORTING OUR RUBBISH

# GOING TO THE TIP

When we have old stuff that we don't want, we might take it to the tip.

I like going to the tip.

Yes, I do.

Sometimes I try on my old clothes, and if they don't fit and nobody wants them, they can go to the tip.

I am not allowed to help Mum at the tip so I stay in the car.

Then we finish with it and come back home.

That's it for now.

Hours 12x2 = 24 hours per day.

Seconds - 60 seconds every minute.

Minutes - 60 minutes every hour.

# MY WATCH

I like my new watch.

I bought it three months ago.

I use my watch to tell the time.

You can see in the picture that my watch has hands.

I am still learning to tell the time.

So far, I understand *quarter to, quarter past* and *half past*. I also know *o'clock*.

I am also learning the 24 hour clock.

I think this story is now finished.

# YOUTUBE

"Come on Megan, tell me about YouTube."

"Wedding," she replies.

I like watching YouTube on my tablet.

Most of the time I watch people dancing at weddings.

I like listening to music, and I am learning to sing.

It is difficult because I don't know many words yet, but I am learning more and more every day.

I also like watching YouTube on my phone.

I think that is it.

VACUUM CLEANER OR HOOVER

# TIDYING MY BEDROOM

"My bedroom is always tidy," says Megan. "All the time!"

"However, it is sometimes a mess," says Simon.

I like having a tidy bedroom— yes I do.

I like my new bedroom in our new house.

It is bigger than my old bedroom and has fewer stairs to get to it.

I like this house because it is on a quiet street.

When we have time, we are going to decorate it. I want it to be pink. It will match my pink, fluffy duvet cover.

A Hole

# Looking Down

Sometimes, in the morning, I make Simon and Mum a cup of tea.

Our dog has his toys all over the floor.

So, I needed to learn to look down so I don't trip over one of his toys.

Before I learned to look down, I would fall over everything. It was a nightmare!

But now, I am learning to look down.

Hopefully, this will stop me from falling into any holes!

"I've got no idea", says Megan.

OPPOSITES

# OPPOSITES

Last year, I started to learn about opposites.

I think the first opposite we talked about was *up* and *down*. We went *up* the hill and *down* the hill in the car.

Soon I learned about *right* and *left*. It took me ages to remember which was *right* and which was *left*.

Now, I think I have it— but I might make the odd mistake!

"I think that it is finished now," says Megan.

Common British Flowers

# FLOWERS

Daffodils, dandelions, daisies, buttercups, and tulips are the names of the flowers I have learned about over the last two years.

I also know about poppies, which are used to remember the soldiers who have died in wars.

Daffodils appear first in springtime, but now they have all gone. Next, we saw dandelions and then daisies. Some gardens have tulips, and now it is mainly buttercups and daisies.

"What is your favourite flower Megan?"

"I don't know," she laughs. "I've got no idea."

DIFFERENT TYPES OF FEELINGS

# EMOTIONS

Emotions are what we feel.

We can feel sad, or happy, or something else. There are lots of different emotions.

When we know the name of the feeling, it helps and stop us from getting frustrated.

"I'm not cross!" Megan might say—even when she *is* cross. It's pretty confusing, for Megan and everybody else!

But as I am learning, things are getting better.

"I think that's it," says Megan.

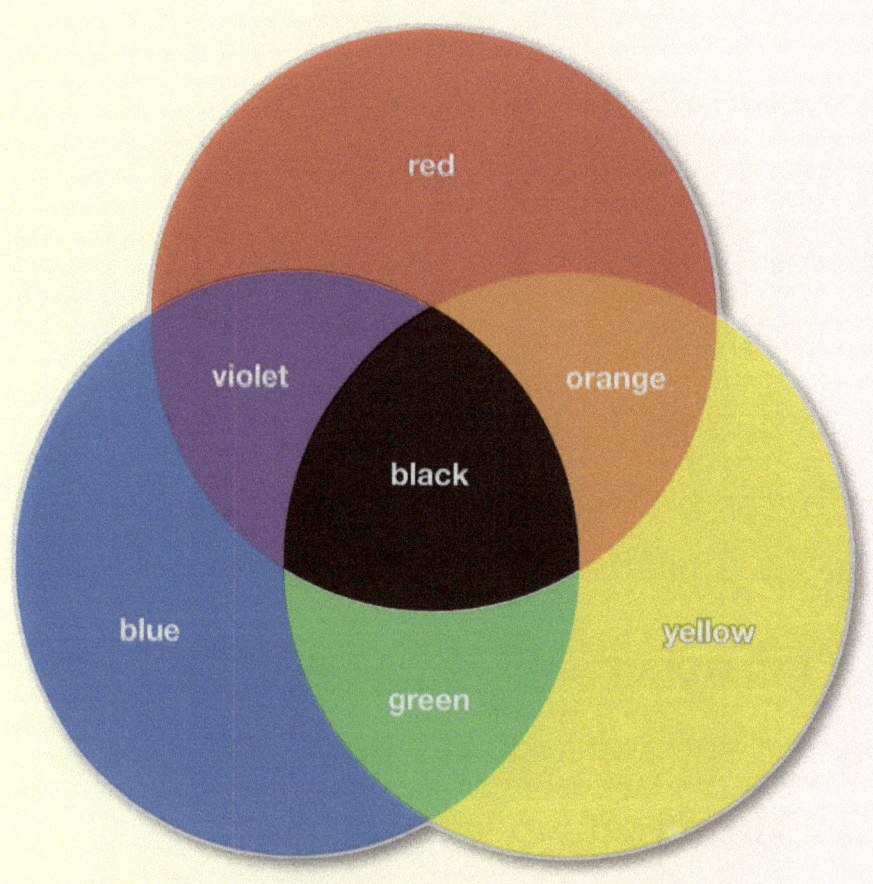

PRIMARY AND SECONDARY COLOURS

# COLOURS

"Shall we write about colours?" asks Simon.

"*Red!*" shouts Megan. "*Green!*"

"You can't just shout colours at me— we need to write a story."

"Simon, I'm not shouting."

"What is your favourite colour, Megan?"

"Purple, pink, orange, yellow, blue."

"Yes, but what is your favourite colour?"

"I don't know. Pink?"

"Tell me something about colour, Megan."

"Your jumper is grey and silver."

"That's enough now!" she says.

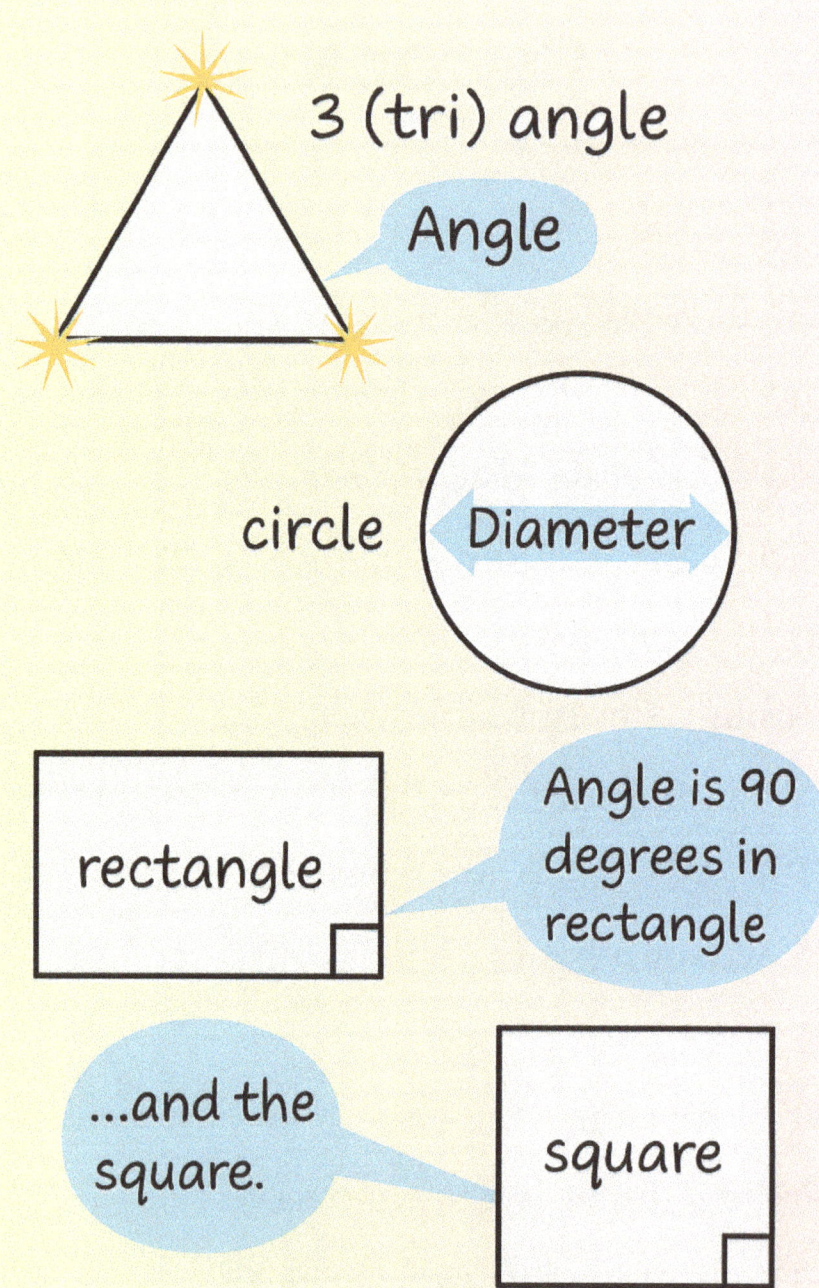

**BASIC 2D SHAPES**

# SHAPES

Triangle, circle, rectangle, square. These are the shapes that I already know.

**Triangle:** has three sides.
**Circle:** has one side.
**Rectangle:** has four sides.
**Square:** has four sides that are all the same length.

I wonder if there are any other shapes that I might want to learn? "Yes, there are," says Simon.

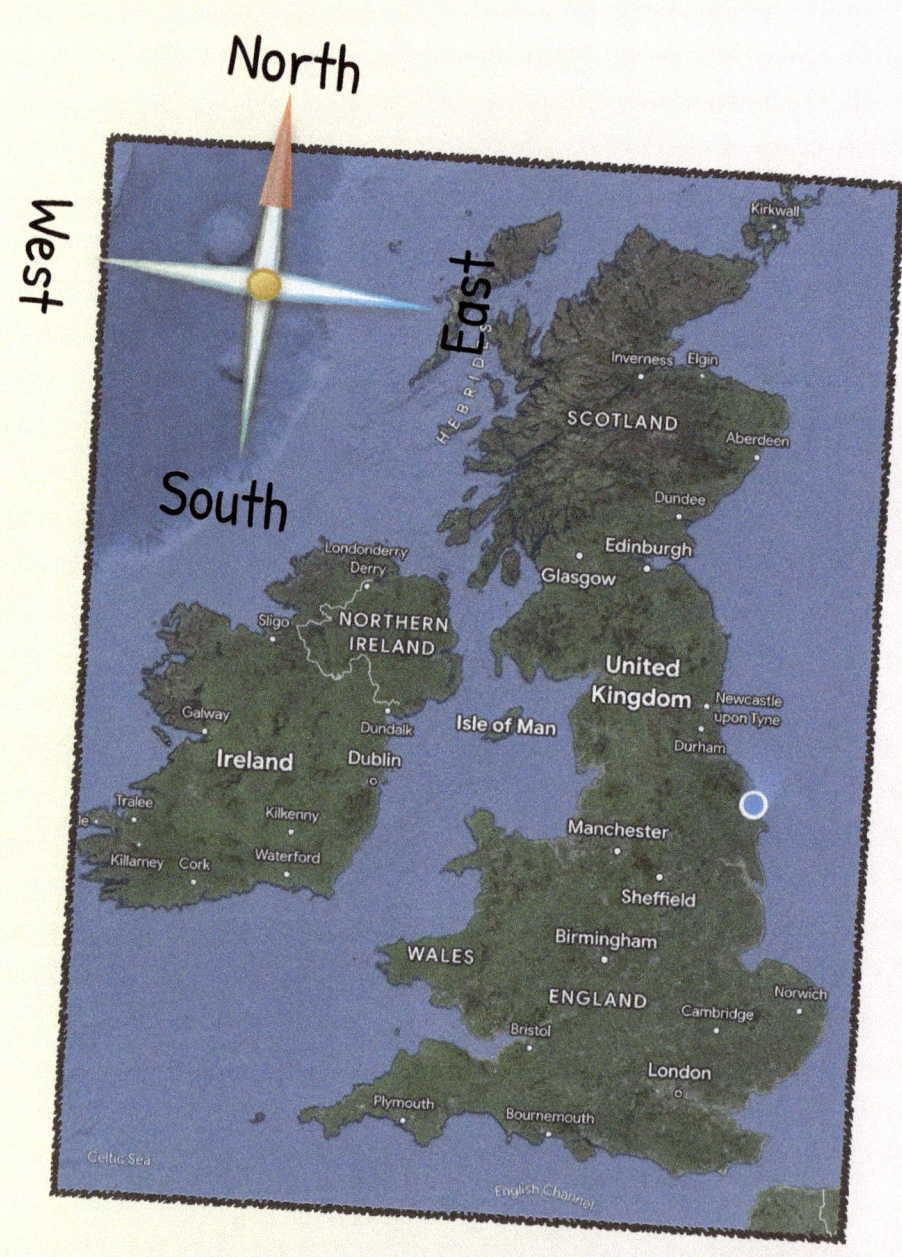

MAP OF THE UNITED KINGDOM

# MAPS

We have been learning about maps.

We have just explored our journey to Pat's house using Google Maps.

It was fun to follow the map from our house to Pat's house.

We saw the towns, villages, and landmarks on the map that we drive past every week.

We even saw our car on the Google satellite view —it was parked outside Pat's house.

Megan was amazed!

👁 we see a rainbow 🌈

👂 we hear a bell 🛎

👃 we smell a flower 🌻

👅 we taste a cake 🍰

🙌 we touch a football ⚽

# THE FIVE SENSES

I have learned there are five senses. These are seeing, hearing, smelling, tasting, and touching.

- We see with our eyes.
- We hear with our ears.
- We smell with our nose.
- We taste with our tongue.
- We touch with our body.

I need to wear glasses to see small writing, but I can watch my television without them.

I don't like loud noises or too many people. It scares me. I like chicken tikka, but not hotter curries.

Empty  Half-full  Full

Two halves

one blue ½

one red ½

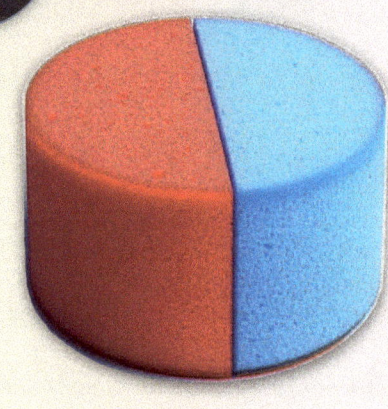

Four Quarters

¼ + ¼ = ½

½ + ½ = whole

# FRACTIONS

The first fraction I learned was ½ (half).

I noticed that sometimes we go to the petrol station and sometimes we don't.

I asked, "Why?"

Simon told me that if the tank that holds diesel is less than half full, we go to get some more.

Then, I counted Simon's sandwiches — he has two sandwiches, each cut in half, which makes four halves.

Now, I am learning that half of a half is a quarter.

"*Hmph,*" - says Megan.

# DIFFERENT TYPES OF CARS

The first car I learned to recognise was a Peugeot. This is a car that is made in France.

Next, I learned about the Mini, which is made in the United Kingdom - U.K.

Mum has a Ford, which is made in America.

Sometimes I see a small Fiat (Italy) and might think this is a Mini until I get a better look.

I am also learning about Audi and BMW, which are both made in Germany.

I like sports cars and also I am learning to spot classic cars—old cars that have been looked after really well.

A Pint of Guinness

# A Story about Beer

I would like to talk to you about beer.

My favourite beer is Guinness. Sometimes I like to have a glass of Guinness after dinner.

When it is all gone, I take my empty glass downstairs.

Then, I put it in the dishwasher.

On Sundays, I go to Pat's house. There, I might have a very small glass of white wine with my lunch. I like going to Pat's house.

I like Guinness. What can I say?

Yes, I do.

SHOPPING BAGS

# SHOPPING

"Shopping for stuff!" Megan says.

I like going shopping with my own money. I like to buy ice-cold coffee with my bank card.

I don't like sharing my basket with Mum.

"Get your own basket, Mum!"

I like to share sometimes but I also like shopping by myself. Mum still has to watch me. She keeps an eye on me.

The End.

"Megan is getting better at writing these stories by herself!" says Simon.

A Blue Letterbox?

# "No, It's Wrong!"

Megan, at first, would say anything!

"That car is big," she might say, pointing at a small car.

So...

We needed a new game.

Now, Simon might say something that is wrong on purpose to see if Megan notices.

"Wrong!" she shouts.

(I don't shout Simon!)

"Look at that blue postbox."

"No! Wrong! It is red!" she responds.

She is getting better every day.

# NEW SANDALS

My old sandals hurt my feet.

But... two weeks ago, I got some new ones.

Mum picked me up from college and said,

"Hey Megan, shall we go and see your sister?"

My sister works in a shoe shop, and I was happy to go and see her. She showed me some sandals that were on sale.

I am glad I went with Mum because now I have some new sandals for the summer.

I think that is it.

# ORDERING TAKE AWAY

# TAKE AWAY

Occasionally, about once a fortnight, we have takeaway food for dinner.

I use my phone to look through the menus that are available on the delivery app.

Sometimes I like to get a fish burger from McDonald's, but I also like the Swiss Mushroom cheeseburger from the Food Shack.

In the past, I used to also get a chocolate milkshake, but now I have iced coffee at home, which I get from Aldi

"I think that is it," says Megan.

I'M NOT CROSS

# BEING TIRED

Sometimes, when I'm tired, my eyes water.

I'm not cross, or angry—*I'm just tired.*

I can tell that I'm getting tired because I start yawning!

In the past, I used to get grumpy, because I was tired and didn't know how to say it.

I am very tired now.

Good night!

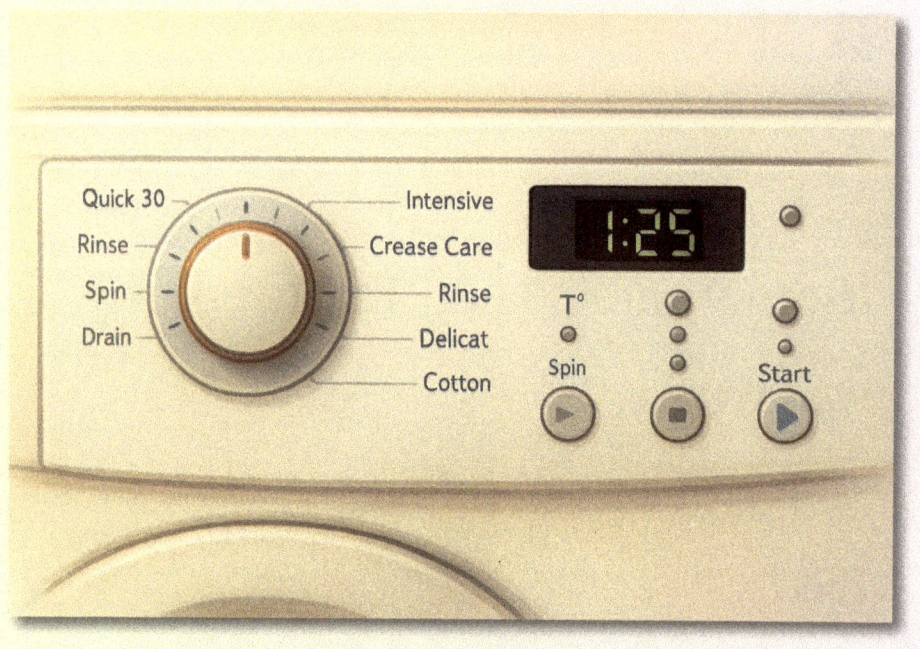

1. Select Quick 30
2. Select Intensive
3. Select Crease Care
4. Select Spin 1200
5. Select Temp 40°C
6. Press Start ▶⏸

# LAUNDRY

Megan is excited to learn to do her own laundry. She has already learned to sort her clothes into those that are dirty and need washing, and those that are clean and can be put away.

*First*, she needs to learn how to sort her clothes into whites and colours.

*Second*, because of our hard water, she needs to use two laundry pods for each wash which she puts in with the washing.

*Third*, she needs to find the right program on the washing machine.

For the moment, Megan knows she needs to ask for help until she fully understands.

# The Third Digit

Megan is getting pretty good at numbers but struggles when they have more than two digits. So, the best thing is to take things slowly.

The third digit from the left is called the *hundreds*. One of the buses we see on our journeys is the number 128.

1 is the third digit so we say one hundred and twenty-eight.

The fourth digit is for the *thousands*—but we will get to that!

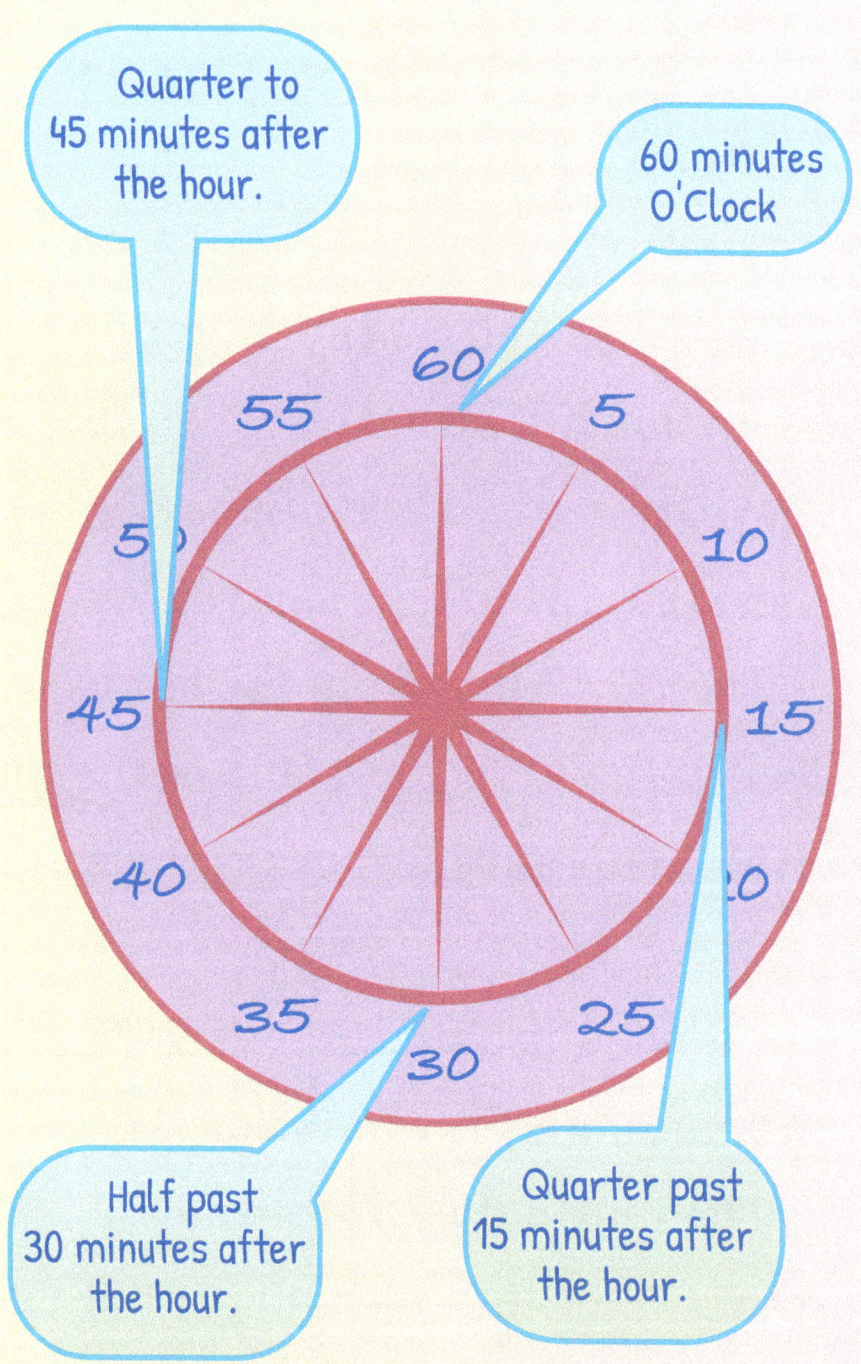

# SIXTY

"Did you know that there are sixty minutes in every hour?" asks Simon?

"*Sixty every hour?*" Megan replies.

"Yes, there are sixty—and did you know that there are sixty seconds in every minute?"

"*I don't know what you're talking about!*"

"Then we have some new things to learn, haven't we?"

"*Yeah...*" sighs Megan!

Plenty of drinks.

Stay in the shade out of the sun.

Cool Clothes.

Keeping Cool With a Fan

## TOO HOT

"So Megan, what shall we write about?"

Ooaghhh... she replies.

"It's too hot, isn't it? Was it hot at college today?"

"Yes. It was too hot for dancing. I just watched YouTube on my phone."

"Don't worry—it's meant to be getting cooler tomorrow."

"Not tomorrow—Monday!" shouts Megan, then she giggles.

**Wet** **Hot**

**Cold** **Dry**

# THE WEATHER

"*What is your favourite weather, Megan?*"

"Sunshine. **Sunshine**! No raining. No snowing."

"*Do you not like snow then?*"

"No. It's too much."

"*Why is it too much?*"

"Because it's too cold."

"*So you like it when it's warm?*"

"Yeah, even when it's hot. I think that's it from me."

Amazon Fire Stick

Remote Control

# MY NEW TELEVISION

I have got a new television.

Well, it's not brand new—it's Mum's old television.

But it's much better than my old one.

My new TV is bigger and I can control it using just one remote control. My old TV is too small and needs to go back to the caravan.

What TV programmes or films do you like Megan?

"I do not know. It's finished now!" she says.

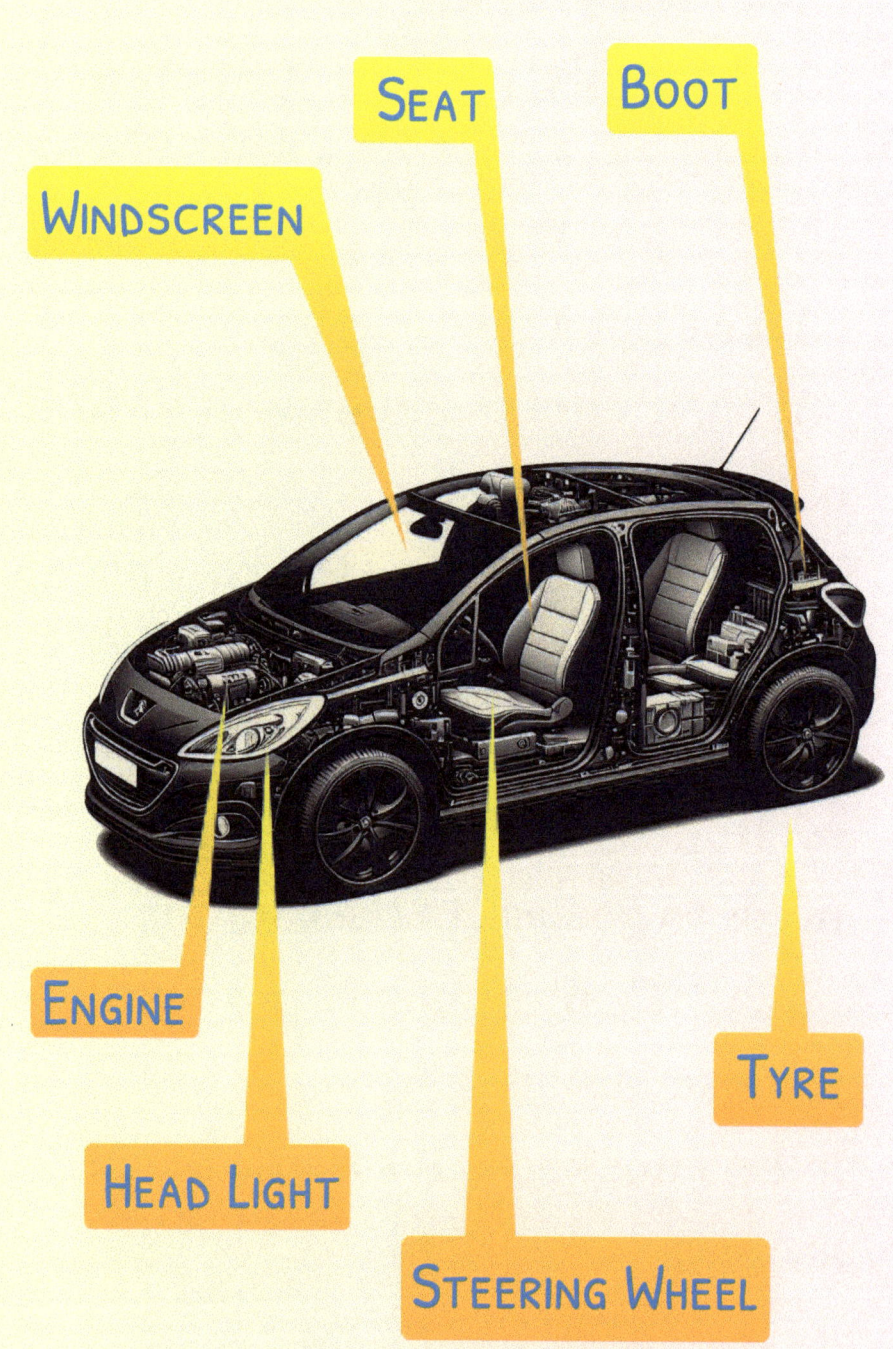

## TAKING A LOOK AT THE CAR

Our car is making a funny noise.

So today, after college, I went with Simon to Kwik Fit, a garage that helps with problems with cars. We asked them to take a look at the car.

As they did this, we went for a walk and got Simon's beard trimmed. I watched YouTube on my phone whilst we waited.

Then we went to pick up the car and came back home.

That's enough of it for now.

# MY NEW WARDROBE

I have a new *wardrobe*.

I am still learning how to say "*wardrobe*." It was pretty confusing for everybody at first, as it's quite a difficult word.

I am keeping my tin of words on the top shelf of my new *wardrobe*.

Next, I just need a new bed.

"I think that's it," says Megan as she taps on the notepad.

## TIME AND DATE

| **Time** | **The Week** |
|---|---|
| Second | Monday |
| Minute | Tuesday |
| Hour | Wednesday |
| Day | Thursday |
| Week | Friday |
| Month | Saturday |
| Year | Sunday |

## Months

January
February
March
April
May
June
July
August
September
October
November
December

## The Seasons

Spring
Summer
Autumn
Winter

## New Words

Birthday
Calendar
Clock
Watch

## NUMBERS AND MATHS

Units

Tens

Hundreds

Thousands

Half

Quarter

Whole

Double

Add

Take-away

Equal

One

Two

Three

Four

Five

Six

Seven

Eight

Nine

Ten

## WEATHER AND NATURE

| **WEATHER** | **NATURE** |
|---|---|
| Sun | Flower |
| Rain | Grass |
| Snow | Tree |
| Wind | River |
| Cloud | Sea |
| Storm | Mountain |
| Rainbow | Garden |
| Sky | Field |

## COLOURS AND SHAPES

| **COLOURS** | **SHAPES** |
|---|---|
| **R**ed | **C**ircle |
| **B**lue | **S**quare |
| **Y**ellow | **T**riangle |
| **G**reen | **R**ectangle |
| **P**ink | **O**val |
| **P**urple | **S**ide |
| **O**range | **C**orner |
| **B**rown | **L**ine |
| **B**lack | |
| **W**hite | |

# HOME

| ROOMS | FURNITURE |
|---|---|
| Kitchen | Bed |
| Bedroom | Chair |
| Bathroom | Table |
| Living room | Cupboard |
| Dining room | Wardrobe |
| Hall | Lamp |
| Utility room | Curtain |
|  | Rug |

| | |
|---|---|
| Shoes | Bread |
| Sandals | Milk |
| Boots | Water |
| Socks | Juice |
| Trousers | Tea |
| Coat | Coffee |
| Shirt | Burger |
| Dress | Chips |
| Hat | Salad |
| Scarf | Cake |
| Gloves | Fruit |
| Bag | Vegetable |
| Umbrella | Meal |
| | Plate |
| | Cup |
| | Spoon |

## People and Feelings

| | |
|---|---|
| Mum | Happy |
| Dad | Sad |
| Sister | Tired |
| Brother | Cross |
| Grandad | Scared |
| Aunty | Angry |
| Uncle | Calm |
| Friend | Excited |
| Teacher | Worried |

## PLACES & TRANSPORT

| | |
|---|---|
| **H**ome | **C**ar |
| **H**ouse | **B**us |
| **R**oad | **T**rain |
| **S**treet | **B**ike |
| **T**own | **P**lane |
| **C**ity | **B**oat |
| **C**ountry | **T**axi |
| **M**ap | **B**ridge |

# Learning & Technology

Book

Page

Pencil

Word

Letter

Sentence

Learn

Think

Phone

Tablet

Television

Remote

App

Internet

Screen

# LEARNING CARDS

Downloadable pdf here:-

*http://drsimonrobinson.com/learning-cards/*

| be | in |
|---|---|
| and | to |
| of | have |
| a | too |

"She is **in** her room."

"Will you **be** my friend?"

"Let's go **to** the park."

"You **and** I will always be friends."

"I **have** a few questions."

"Today is the first **of** November."

"That's **too** much."

"I saw **a** bear today."

| | |
|---|---|
| it | you |
| I | he |
| that | with |
| for | on |

"**You** are really nice."

"**It** is sunny outside."

"**He** is my brother."

"**I** really like it here."

"I want to go **with** you."

"**That** door is open."

"I watch movies **on** my tablet."

"This letter is **for** you."

| do | at |
|---|---|
| say | but |
| this | we |
| they | his |

"Can you pick me up **at** the shops?"

"What will you **do** now?"

"I'm sorry **but** she's away."

"Can I **say** something?"

"**We** are going to watch a movie."

"**This** is my favourite beer."

"This is **his** box."

"**They** are here!"

| from | won't |
|------|-------|
| that | by |
| not | she |
| can't | or |

"I **won't** open it."

"This card came **from** my sister."

"Will you come **by** and see me?"

"**That** is a really cool trick!"

"**She** is very happy."

"It's **not** my fault!"

"Do you like blue **or** yellow?"

"I **can't** open it.

| | |
|---|---|
| as | can |
| what | who |
| go | get |
| their | if |

"What **can** I do for you?"

"I try to be **as** quiet as possible."

"**Who** can help me?"

"**What** are you thinking of?"

"Can you **get** me my glasses?"

"I want to **go** there."

"What **if** I am late?"

"This is **their** house."

| would | make |
|---|---|
| her | about |
| all | know |
| my | will |

"Shall we **make** something?"

"**Would** you help me?"

"What is this movie **about**?"

"I have **her** book."

"Do you **know** where this place is?"

"**All** my favourite books are on this shelf."

"I **will** help you find that place."

"**My** Mum is coming to visit."

| | |
|---|---|
| as | there |
| up | year |
| one | so |
| time | think |

| | |
|---|---|
| "That is your coat, over **there**." | "**As** soon as she's here, I'll talk to her." |
| "What are your plans for next **year**?" | "**Up** the hill." |
| "I am **so** sorry." | "She is **one** of my teachers." |
| "I **think** I need a lie down." | "What **time** is dinner?" |

| | | |
|---|---|---|
| shoe | duck | dog |
| socks | horse | frog |
| hat | monkey | pig |
| cap | chicken | rabbit |
| gloves | bee | cow |
| trainers | seal | snail |

| | | |
|---|---|---|
| boots | tiger | worm |
| trousers | zebra | snake |
| T-shirt | elephant | fish |
| blouse | giraffe | sheep |
| shorts | mouse | fly |
| bikini | crab | butterfly |

| | | |
|---|---|---|
| scarf | tortoise | fox |
| knickers | swan | peacock |
| flipflop | squirrel | parrot |
| glasses | suitcase | purse |
| umbrella | satchel | backpack |
| plant | sunglasses | handbag |

| ball | egg | apple |
| --- | --- | --- |
| car | butter | orange |
| guitar | bacon | lemon |
| headphones | chips | pear |
| drum | pizza | banana |
| taxi | sandwich | strawberry |

| tractor | noodles | cherry |
| --- | --- | --- |
| van | rice | tomato |
| bus | cake | chili |
| motorbike | pie | cucumber |
| bicycle | milk | potato |
| scooter | coffee | onion |

| plane | beer | carrot |
|---|---|---|
| train | wine | sweetcorn |
| rocket | salt | cheese |
| boat | rainbow | shell |
| helicopter | cloud | sun |
| traffic light | star | moon |

| map | clock | paperclip |
| --- | --- | --- |
| castle | bulb | pen |
| tent | key | book |
| house | door | pencil |
| watch | bed | letter |
| phone | chair | pin |

| | | |
|---|---|---|
| spanner | screwdriver | barrel |
| saw | magnet | hammer |
| brick | chain | cog |
| knife | axe | telescope |
| tap | toilet | toilet roll |
| sponge | toothbrush | bath |

| | | |
|---|---|---|
| mirror | bell | bucket |
| window | cart | balloon |
| doughnut | burger | hotdog |
| mountain | bus stop | microphone |
| plug | battery | volcano |
| mouth | eye | tooth |

| nose | ear | tongue |
| --- | --- | --- |
| red | blue | green |
| yellow | pink | purple |
| white | black | orange |
| brown | grey | happy |
| sick | angry | sad |

119

# AFTERWARD

The primary purpose of this book is to provide an engaging tool that will help Megan develop her reading skills. Megan is a young adult and dislikes anything that is clearly for children. By creating a book that is deeply relevant it is hoped she will remain engaged and develop her reading and verbal comprehension.

It is possible that other young adults with a learning disability might find this book useful. With this in mind I thought I'd briefly outline my strategy in helping Megan develop her verbal and written comprehension. Whilst I am reluctant to consider myself any sort of authority in learning disability, my background includes a deep understanding of the mind through experience in psychology, psychiatry, neurology, hypnotherapy and Buddhism.

## A SENSE OF BEING

Every time our mind recognises a 'thing' it creates the sense of an observer, of this 'thing'. A sense of being is dependent upon a continuous state of perceiving things in our senses and thoughts. This perception needs labels - the names of various objects in our environment. Without knowing concepts such as time, date and number we remain disorientated towards many daily experiences which fosters helplessness and dependence. The more labels we know, the more we experience a sense of being.

If we have multiple impaired senses then this process of object recognition through labelling is challenging - the mind finds it difficult to isolate the object from its environment and it takes greater repetition and patience for concepts to solidify. Once this happens then understanding arises but it just takes much more time for those with difficulties.

## The importance of number

Knowing that seven is a bigger number than six takes time. Initially this involves repetition to install the first 10 numbers. I taught Megan the card game called *Patience* (here in the UK, *Solitaire* is another name for the game). This was a great way to install the order of these numbers. About five years after teaching Megan *Patience* she surprised us by completing the game on her phone - it takes time - 'patience' is definitely a pertinent term! So it's not important that one masters *patience*, more an appreciation that numbers exist in a definite order.

Numbers are quite abstract and it took time for Megan to establish a confident understanding of even just the first twenty or so.

# Our Road Sign Game

In order to develop (and test) Megan's grasp of numbers we used familiar road signs whenever we were out in the car. On our journeys I could ask 'How far to Scarborough?' and we would have multiple opportunities with differing numbers to test her comprehension. We gradually moved on to asking what is the next number beyond the one we read, we learned to 'add one.'

# Verbal learning

Initially, in order to expand Megan's knowledge of nouns, it took lots of repetition. This helped Megan learn to pronounce various consonants, which gradually improved her speech clarity. During the covid lockdowns we had plenty of time and we used coins and playing cards to develop concepts of number, and a black board to start to explore words. Although I wasn't aware of it at this time, Megan's learning here was predominantly verbal, despite her watching and occasionally seeming to recognise words.

# Orientation

Once Megan had a grasp of number we could start to teach her about time and date. This was highly repetitive and very gradual - however, over a course of about three years she began to grasp the basics. It is only recently she can confidently list the names of the months. We are keen that Megan reaches the greatest degree of independence possible - and for this she needs to be orientated in time. Using her phone's calendar app and populating this with important dates such as family members birthdays was very useful. With this, she felt a certain empowerment in 'knowing' some basic facts and further motivated her to understand dates.

## FORESIGHT

Once Megan began to gain a sense of orientation in time and a working volume of nouns she started to think about things. She developed foresight and could plan her actions in a very simple manner. She was still very limited, however, we took this as a very motivating and positive sign.

## BASIC WORD RECOGNITION

On our regular journeys there were a number of businesses we drove past that had signs that displayed either 'open' or 'closed'. We developed a game where I would ask if the shop was open or closed. Megan guessed an awful lot initially. The perception of these words was a challenge and it took several months before Megan was confident. Even then she would occasionally guess and needed prompting with 'Are you sure?'

Her perception was developing yet it seemed that her attention was variable and she simply couldn't see what she was looking at. Most of the time she simply remembered and failed to notice when open had become closed and vice versa.

## OUR WORDS GAME

I searched for the top 200, most frequently used English words. We printed these out and made some laminated cards. On the opposite side of each card we had a simple sentence that utilised the word. I also made some cards with a picture on one side using emoji and the word on the opposite side of the card.

We have been using these word cards for about two years. Our game has evolved over this time. Initially it was largely looking at the pictures and once this was recognised we turned it over to show only the word. Then Megan, prompted by already knowing the image could learn to recognise the word. Again, it took patience and repetition.

Eventually we moved to keeping the picture side down from the onset with Megan learning to recognise the word only. It has taken time but gradually she has learned to scan words and try to pronounce them from reading the letters.

If you would like a copy of the learning cards we developed I have made them available as a pdf file on my website. You can find it here:-

http://drsimonrobinson.com/learning-cards/

# Next steps

My goal is to continue 'populating' Megan's mind with words. Her capacity to grasp things is improving and with this her confidence. Her focus is very variable and we have to keep our learning sessions flexible and fun. I am hoping with the publication of this book we will expand Megan's vocabulary and her reading ability. If this book is useful in achieving these goals then we might continue to write further books to continue this aim.

# Conclusion

Megan has progressed significantly in her understanding and communication. This has resulted in an improvement in both her and our qualities of life. It seems that many 'higher skills' arise through emergence - that is, through increasing her vocabulary she is gaining executive skills and complex thought without these being explicitly taught. Her problem is largely the acquisition of concepts, but, with patience and determination, once she gains these her ability to utilise them seems entirely normal.

# ABOUT THE AUTHORS

Megan is still learning about words, grammar and writing. We have written this book together yet she lacks the necessary insight to give fully informed consent. Whilst needing to keep the content relevant I have also kept any details that might identify her minimal.

My background is Medicine with a speciality in Anaesthesia and General Practice. I ceased practicing medicine in 2012 due to severe depressive illness. I have written several books on mental illness and continue to develop my understanding of the mind through studying ancient philosophies. I am writing a complete course in modern alchemy which aims to demystify this complicated topic.

In addition to my ongoing studies I work with local authors in promoting our work through social media and self-published books. Our group, 'The Wordbotherers' has published five magazines and four books since its inception late last year.

Further information is available from my website and the Wordbotherers website.

- *drsimonrobinson.com* — *Official Author Site*
- *wordbotherers.com* — *Community of Writers and Poets*
- *contact@drsimonrobinson.com* — *Professional email*

# ALL BY MYSELF

## BY MEGAN AND SIMON

After learning the basics of words, time, and numbers in *A Little Bit of Help*, Megan was ready to take her next step — a step toward independence. *All By Myself* continues her journey with stories that explore everyday life as both practice and adventure.

From walking the dog and catching the bus to learning about geography, seasons, and the solar system, each chapter blends real experiences with simple explanations. Megan learns how to plan her day, how money works, and how to manage things that once felt confusing — all through the same mix of humour, repetition, and discovery that made the first book so loved.

The stories gradually grow with her confidence, moving from home and college life into bigger ideas: understanding maps, numbers in context, and even how science helps explain the world. Along the way, familiar themes return — patience, pride, and the joy of doing things for oneself.

Written with compassion, insight, and a deep respect for learning at every pace, *All By Myself* is not just a book about reading; it's about growing — about how small acts of understanding can open entire worlds.

It's a story of progress, independence, and the beautiful truth that learning doesn't end when the lesson does — it continues in every moment of daily life.

**ALL BY MYSELF**
BY MEGAN AND SIMON
COLOUR EDITION - £11.99
AVAILABLE THROUGH :
INGRAM SPARK AND BOOKSHOPS
ISBN: **978-1-0684310-4-3**

# The Phantasmagoria of Seeming

My work brings together the disciplines of medicine, psychology, hypnotherapy, and mysticism, guided by a lifelong inquiry into what truly constitutes a person. Across these fields, I have come to see that much of human suffering arises not from what is, but from what is believed to be. Conventional approaches often treat distress and limitation as conditions belonging to a solid self — a self that can be damaged, healed, or defined. Yet when we begin to see through the illusion of a fixed identity, the landscape changes. What once appeared as injury or deficiency reveals itself instead as habit and pattern, capable of transformation.

This understanding has profound implications, particularly in education and special needs. Rather than viewing someone as broken or incomplete, we can recognise that there is no permanent self that is harmed — only patterns of thought and behaviour shaped by circumstance, trauma, or limitation. These patterns can be gently reshaped. Through patience, example, and repetition, unhelpful habits give way to new ones, allowing natural intelligence and expression to re-emerge. In this light, even physical or intellectual constraints need not define a person; they simply inform the path of adaptation.

At the heart of development lies language — the gradual naming of the world that allows the sense of self to arise. When a child learns to distinguish objects, subjectivity blossoms, and with it comes awareness, imagination, and emotional life. For those whose development is delayed, rebuilding this process begins with words: not exhaustive lists, but vivid, contrasting examples that make concepts clear and alive. Once a class of things is understood — a few mammals, shapes, colours — the mind naturally fills in the rest. Written words deepen this further; once recognised visually, they expand the mind's ability to think and connect.

Emotional growth follows the same path. As self-awareness matures, so does the need for ethical grounding and emotional regulation. For this, I draw upon both Buddhist and Christian traditions — not as dogma, but as complementary guides to compassion, responsibility, and the quiet courage to meet experience as it is. The ultimate aim is not to impose meaning, but to reveal the freedom already present when the illusion of separateness dissolves.

In that freedom, learning — and life itself — becomes not repair, but realisation.

PhantasmogoriaOfSeeming.com

# ABRACADABRA

## (I WILL CREATE AS I SPEAK)

*I have been teaching my step daughter to read.*
*It is an education for both of us.*
*I started with the signs we see on familiar routes.*

*Open. Closed.*
*For Sale.*
*Sold.*

*Oblivious at first, she cannot see what I point at.*
*Reminds me of the Buddhist parable called 'Pointing at the Moon'.*
*Until one understands what 'pointing at' means,*
*one is liable to mistake the finger for the moon.*
*Then, suddenly she sees it.*
*A pattern of letters that means*

*'Open'. 'Closed'.*
*'For sale'.*
*'Sold.'*

*Initially she might cheat and 'remember' rather than recognise the word.*
*But now, she cannot.*
*Closed isn't open and open can't be closed.*
*The word now arises whether she looks for it or not,*
*and subtly imparts its message.*
*Yet, a few weeks ago, there was nothing there at all.*

*Abracadabra!*

www.ingramcontent.com/pod-product-compliance
Lightning Source LLC
Chambersburg PA
CBHW061232070526
44584CB00030B/4092